MW01483888

CONSPIRACY OF LIGHT

Publications

BOOKS BY D.S. MARTIN:
So The Moon Would Not Be Swallowed
Poiema
Conspiracy of Light

BOOKS EDITED BY D.S. MARTIN FOR THE POIEMA POETRY SERIES:
Sydney Lea, *Six Sundays Toward a Seventh*
Paul Mariani, *Epitaphs for the Journey*
Robert Siegel, *Within This Tree of Bones*
Julie L. Moore, *Particular Scandals*
Barbara Crooker, *Gold*
Robert Cording, *A Word in My Mouth*
Luci Shaw, *Scape*

FORTHCOMING:
Tania Runyan, *Second Sky*
John Leax, *Remembering Jesus*
Paul J. Willis, *Say This Prayer into The Past*

Conspiracy of Light

Poems Inspired by the Legacy of C. S. Lewis

To Gordon:

May you always conspire
with the light! *[signature]*

D. S. MARTIN

For Ian
(inscribed in error!)

CASCADE *Books* · Eugene, Oregon

Imprint Here
An Imprint of Wipf and Stock Publishers
199 W. 8th Ave., Suite 3
Eugene, OR 97401

www.wipfandstock.com

ISBN 13: 978-1-62564-286-8

Cataloging-in-Publication data:

D. S. Martin.

    Conspiracy of light : Poems inspired by the legacy of C. S. Lewis / D. S. Martin.

    xii + 110 p.; 23 cm—Includes bibliographical references and index.

    ISBN 13: 978-1-62564-286-8

    1. 2. 3. 4. I. II.

CALL NUMBER 2012

Manufactured in the USA.

"Flamboyance" by D.S. Martin is reprinted by permission from the April 17, 2013, issue of *The Christian Century*. www.christiancentury.org. Copyright © 2013 by *The Christian Century*.

In memory of
Robert Siegel
(1939–2012)

"The Teacher searched to find just the right words, and what he wrote was upright and true."
—Ecclesiastes 12:10

Contents

Contents

PART THREE: What the Poet Sings

PART FOUR: Ready to Re-Ignite

PART FIVE | With New Eyes

Contents

Preface

When I consider how my light advanced, it is most fitting that C.S. Lewis should be an important focus for my poetry. "Fifty years after his death, Lewis remains one of the most influential popular writers of our age", wrote Alister McGrath in his fine new biography. The first reason for *this* book, however, is that C.S. Lewis is one of the most influential writers—of any time period—on me. There was a time in my youth when I would buy and read any and every book I discovered by C.S. Lewis. What I had found was that he wrote in a way that engaged my mind like no other writer. He was respected in a variety of fields, and held passionately to his faith in Christ. Years later, when I began re-reading his books I was surprised to find many of the ideas I'd held as my own, had been planted by Lewis. It's true, that not all of his arguments stand up as well as I had earlier thought. Despite the imprint of the era in which he wrote, there's a timeless wisdom in his writing that continues to enrich any who are open to it.

As I re-read Lewis I was also re-introduced to his exceptional skill at presenting ideas through analogy. Many of the poems in this book began with the poet in me taking a Lewis word-picture and pushing it in one direction or another until it took on a life of its own.

Each of the poems in *Conspiracy of Light* springs directly from something Lewis wrote, or from events in his life. The source for some will be obvious, even to casual readers of Lewis. The notes at the end of this book, although unnecessary for reading the poems, direct readers back to the source material. I would be pleased if my poems expand readers' appreciation of Lewis and bring them back to his work.

Preface

November 22nd of this year marks the fiftieth anniversary of the death of C.S. Lewis. His is a legacy that will continue to grow as the years pass. Here I honour him, and the one for whom he wrote.

Soli Deo Gloria,
DSM

PART ONE
From a Deep Well of Memory

Of This & Other Worlds

A glance over your shoulder
      assures you   you can always get back
            should this white wood overwhelm you
Fat   wet   flakes descend slowly through the stillness
      A flickering light beckons & you walk forward
            snow pressed beneath your every step
All things are possible here   Times intertwine
      You might find a lamppost in the forest
            you might meet a faun a goat man
      who invites you to tea & by his blazing fire
tells of naiads & dryads dancing
            through the midnights of long ago
      He may play his pipe & lull you
into sleep's other realm
            Much later   when you return to the familiar
      & even the flutter of pages has ceased
are you not seized with longing?

The Longing

for C.S. Lewis

It came to him
    staring toward the Castlereagh Hills
    from an upstairs window

It came to him
    from a homemade toy garden
    in the lid of a biscuit tin

It came from the sight of steamers
    down below in Belfast Lough
    & the sound of a ship's horn at night

It came from the interior space
    of the rambling house his father designed
    (rooms filled with books & long book-lined
    passages leading to empty sunlit places
    books piled in the attic & two-deep
    in the book case on the landing)
    where the distant sounds of pipes
    of gurgling cisterns & of the wind's breath
    would wind through corridors to find
    him beside the comforting fire

It came most perhaps from the loss of his mother
    first through dire illness & finally through death
    the longing for longing the desire for desire

Proof

Small feet find the ground solid
small hands learn to open & close doors
Words take on meaning
lifted & sifted   begin to prove   disprove
form a net to catch & hold   enough
of what is   to scratch at understanding

The ground is solid   rough   cold
a bicycle skids out in gravel
pink palms get scraped   & sting
Some things are real enough   A kid's
heart clings   until a mother's cancer
overwhelms hope   & answers unravel

To face the horrible present   & long
for the out-of-reach   end-of-term
idyllic blue horizon   teaches desire
teaches wait   When his one life gets replaced
on a small scale   it's easier to anticipate
all things made new

He began   as a pagan   with pangs
of woe & yearning   & tales
of dead gods rising every spring
Could all this longing mean nothing?
His path to salvation was well-worn
but only by those walking away

When he proved the unprovable   he moved
those on his side   & proved himself
the greater debater   but did he win?
Some things   are only known
once you step in   Later he learned
how hearts have logic of their own

5

Burned & frozen by contradictions
that seem equally true   comforted
by your own voice   & tricks of the tongue
you blind yourself   as I do
When the mind has a choice   we find
the heart's already chosen

Silent Walks

Walking and talking are two very great pleasures,
but it is a mistake to combine them.

    What could mute Lewis   make him shun talk
besides submersion in his work   would be
the opportunity to walk
    Every day he could   he would
slip out alone after lunch
    Every January   he & Warnie
took three-or-four-day tramps   through damp
marshes   across windy downs
not speaking   not smoking
their senses alert for stirring vistas   for silence
for meaningful sounds
    Every spring he was accompanied
by such as Tolkien
& Barfield   friends who'd wisely yield
to stillness   wordlessly share
their appreciation of a landscape
or the shape of a light-tinged cloud   & save chatter
& that sound of male laughter   for after
they'd come to their pub for the night
like Frodo & friends at the *Prancing Pony*
in Bree-town
    Is it any wonder   Lewis put Ransom
where we first see him   after a thundershower
under the drip of a chestnut tree?

Broadcast Talks

C.S. Lewis on BBC Radio circa 1942

      Listening to radio recordings from long
before my birth   from this side of the Atlantic
it's hard to imagine the man
      His unhurried   big-jowled voice
like a bassoon's steady grasp
on a composer's steadily growing theme
the cultured sound   his mouth   round
moves slower   & wider   for vowels
      His voice insists
each   should   be   drawn   out
dispensing deep thoughts
from a deep well of memory
      The voice of an Oxford don
sedate compared with his *hoom tum toom*
in the lecture room
with a hint (some say) of Ulster
a well-articulated murmur where Rs
assert themselves   down the precise slope
of his arguments   until worn smooth
to make way   for yawning ahs
      Coming from anoth(ah)   time & place
this man   long buried   explains eternity

Oxford Diptych

1) Oxford Downpour

Still   I hear the gush of rushing runoff
along the cobblestones

Still picture
the ambulation of black umbrellas
between colleges   as rain falls
darkening Oxford streets

My preoccupation isn't shelter   or wanting to eat
but coming to this particular pub
where Lewis   Tolkien & Williams used to meet
where their banter   & maybe even
a celebrated story read aloud
has soaked into the walls

We've been allowed   time enough
for a meal & drink
to take in   the patrons' din
the clink of glasses   the clatter of plates
& to stare   a little too late
at frames & fixtures

2) Magdalen College

From the sitting room   the muffled clack   of Warnie's typewriter
punches through a closed door
You might also hear Jack   splash at the washstand
in his plain bedroom   or tread across the floor
The shabby armchairs   draped with musty covers   never cleaned
have absorbed years of tobacco & dust   among other things
Behind the faded grey chesterfield
is a worn table   scraped & scarred   the board of the rings
marked by absent glasses   ink bottles & enamel beer jug   marred
by cigarette burns & ink stains   & holding a pot of tea

It's all in contrast with the high-ceiling & panelled walls
& with the golden   shining mulberry tree
you see   this morning   in the grove from Lewis's window
as foot-falls approach up the stairs & through the hall
Soon you're part of the laughter
after Tolkien's filled his pipe from his pouch
stretched out on the couch   & held a match to its bowl
He compares this to life in the Shire
while Warnie adds coal to the fire
& Jack flicks his ashes wherever they may fall

Hedonics

while travelling by tube from Paddington to Harrow

Every lighted house seen from the road is magical
& like distant music   calls with a voice
you may cling to   or ignore
seeks your attention   like the flickering compartment
of some parallel ghost train
rumbling through unattainable neighbourhoods

In each window someone sits down to a fine dinner
a good conversation   a good book   or to scrape
a few scraps together   to be eaten in solitude
with no awareness of your passing
but then you   or that someone   or a pedestrian in between
looks up   at the blinking jet overhead
to consider *those* passengers   travelling high
over distant hills   distant hills which are blue
even if   when seen up close appear green

You then choose   whether you know it or not
whether you will surrender
to those inner revelries   that wordlessly wing
toward you   simultaneously from distant past
& distant future   & want you to sing
as with a burning choir   of joy

An Aversion to Film

There is death in the camera
—C.S. Lewis, "On Stories"

       The room grows black & a beam from the back
projects monochromatic film images
Jack Lewis has been dragged out to a movie It's 1938
He squirms in his seat not wanting to look
There's an irrelevant young woman in shorts
He splutters *She's not in the book*
In the story he knows the three cohorts
(minus the girl) are about to suffocate
in the mummified kings' tomb creating
a mythopoetic atmosphere of claustrophobic doom
But here it's exchanged for the cinematic thrill
of instant earthquake & a subterranean volcanic boom
       In 1956 he suspects another novel he's read
has been undermined as a film
by having a love story intertwined
       What do you think he's said
(considering his knowledge of the Norse)
of the depiction by Disney of dwarfs?
       How do you think Jack might react
to *his* writing on the screen with fighting between
two of his characters twisted into rivals
& an invented teen love scene? A silhouette
slips out the back as a matter of survival

Surprise by Joy

It was just like Jack
He'd not got   years earlier   how Tolkien
was jealous of his friendship with Charles Williams   & he'd not
fought back   when he'd been made
an unpaid scullery maid
Warnie thought obvious   what Joy sought
through her transatlantic trip
Jack was oblivious
& felt chivalrous   a civil marriage so they couldn't shove
her out of the country   How strange   such a genius
could be surprised   after the fact   by love
Long before Lewis caught on   her ploy worked
& his colleagues smirked   *He's been doubly*
surprised by Joy

Grief Observed

Sorrow is a cat   crouching in the undergrowth
often undetected   Her habits have worn a path
uniquely into each life   firm footholds from childhood
We don't see her approach   & then we can't see past
obscured by darkness & overgrowth

Like thick black paint obscuring a masterpiece
like the gradual onset of darkness   like a door
slammed in your face   like a creature's impulse to crawl
into its shell to hide   like an enemy bomber circling overhead
sorrow can't easily be pushed aside

PART TWO
More than Somewhat Like That

Extrapolations

Long grass sways
pine branches swing
cumulus clouds race across the sky

Imagine we see more than these things
even the wind itself

Imagine our love is more than a grimy
reflection of something greater

Dust swirls
in a sunbeam
Imagine we see more
even the light itself

Imagine our analogies & extrapolations
are more than somewhat like that

The Sacred Fish

You can't desire to catch the sacred fish
as much as he desires to be caught
& yet
he darts through the dim depths
with tail swerve & swish
laughs with the joy of glistening fins
at huge holes in your net
through which he swims

To get the shining coin from his mouth
is worth selling all you have
To get *him* even better
Everything you know about him
wavers in uneven light

Just below the surface
so it's barely wet
you let down your net
as he dives to the bottom
You seek the depths
as he leaps through waves
You search the shallows
as he heads for open water
& your tattered nets come up empty

If you let him
he'll repair them himself
trim knotted clumps   & untie tangles
Selecting the right fibres
he'll tear & twist
the sinews of your heart into fine mesh
stretch them as thin as a pin
as wide as your whole being
a needle-shimmer piercing your soul

Better is one day in his boats
than thousands elsewhere

Bottle

As pure beams of morning infiltrate your window
the cut-glass bottle   high on the ledge   cannot be hid
It catches light   dazzles   reflects   refracts
but cannot hold it   Placed under a bushel
dark emptiness is immediate & complete

I know whoever's not against us is for us
& whoever's not with us is against us
Light glints off the glass in different ways

I know he blessed the peacemakers
yet came   to bring a sword   taught
love your enemies   yet hate
father   mother   wife   children

It's *like trying to bottle a sunbeam*
Some subtleties splash from the rim
& splatter the ceiling
its substance overflows the brim
& puddles the floor
Even what clearly brightens the interior
beautifully makes its escape
diffused through the glass brightly

The Coinage of Your Brian

Thoughts are like coins   that spill
from our pockets   onto a foreign hotel dresser
the inscription & sovereign's image
worn thin
      Minted in the basements
of our minds   they imitate perceived worth
but are of questionable currency
in the coffee shop
      I'd like to think   (cha-ching cha-ching)   that if thoughts
were coins   philosophers & poets would be millionaires
& we'd be paid   more directly
for our evening prayers
      But I have thoughts I'd not want to jingle my pocket long
thirty tarnished pieces of silver   daily cast
to the ground   each cast with my own shameful effigy
& I've printed counterfeit bills   hundreds of them
that caricature the divine in my own image
I'd like to get those out of circulation too
      Perhaps you will forgive my forgeries
& suggest   they point toward what's true

The Possibilities

What did the Professor mean
  Nothing is more probable
when asked of possible worlds
everywhere   just around the corner?

I know how unobservant I can be
of all that's plainly before me
never mind the microscopic   the subatomic
the spiritual   the possibilities
from unimagined dimensions
colours lost in shifting light
shapes obscured by descending darkness
rising fog   a closing door
Might the end of time reveal
all existence as simultaneously real
from the history of each place?

I'm a squid on the ocean floor
unaware of the water
a willow dancing on a creekbank
unconscious of the wind

A small girl tumbles through a wardrobe
into a wood filled with unbelievable truth
a parallel world   She has proven herself
reliable   Why should we not believe her?

If A Poet

If a poet were to write a river
he'd have it descend from distant highlands
start as a weak trickle   then grow stronger
flow straight down   then slow into winding bends
It would conform to the norm of river
hungry to undercut the outside bank
& broaden   the way a tree gets thicker
moving down from leaf tip   to limb   to trunk
It would submit to leave its deposit
sediment sinking where the river slows
on the inside of the curve   until it
pours gifts on the poor   & a sandbank grows

If a poet were to scratch a homestead
onto paper   from the nib of his pen
furrows would spread across the countryside
like a calendar picture over June
His cornfield would grow taller all summer
stalks breathing their secrets along the rows
of a bumper crop before September
or of a plague of locust on the news
If he exposed himself to such trials
not letting himself escape   might it prove
to his neighbours he accepts the troubles
such as all other characters receive?

If a poet were to live for a time
within his work   he would honour the splash
of the swirling world so that his poem
would leap the banks   beyond the glare & swish
of page   or stage   & even as the writer
would face the rising water   He would
warn neighbours not to build on the flood plain
but come to the aid of any who did

If the bridge were to wash out   he'd accept
the problem of being cut off from town
himself   but may revise things to permit
that some hero got through   & did not drown

Canine Inquiry

She would sniff her way through your possessions
The presence of dog cat sweat gasoline meat
would decide your obsessions She'd assume you eat
as she does & your tastes are mere appetite
cinnamon or sonata All she has
to compare with your intellectual pursuits
is her focus on chasing & chewing
a rubber ball or watching a squirrel
scamper a wall Wouldn't the best guess
of a mongrel scholar about your life
be a chasing of her tail? Better for her
to take you at your word to wag her tail in assent
& snarl her scepticism at growling sceptics
who've never walked at your heel

The Dogs

If I creep carefully through the house
the dogs might stay put
They're not asleep   they never sleep
they keep their eyes on me
I'd sooner just let them be
& suggest   you should too
We can make ourselves believe
they don't exist   or are easily dismissed
but there's a gruff muffled growl
that keeps us from moving forward
anticipating the ruff gripe & howl
& the jawsnap   He said   they don't bite
but I think that's under ideal conditions
if it be his will   & all that
They're not asleep   they never sleep
they keep their eyes on you
Here   let me show you   hidden beneath
as I   roll up my sleeve   the scrapes
& deep scars from their vicious teeth

I want to tell them to move
to pick them up and throw them into the sea
like a mustard tree
or a handful of mountain   but they won't move
They keep guarding the doorway
They're not asleep   they never sleep
they keep their eyes on me

Metaphor

... *if we are going to talk about things which are not perceived by the senses, we are forced to use language metaphorically.*

—*C.S. Lewis*

I place an idea before you   & you kick it around a bit
its thud & spin & balance
respectful   trying to not sully or smudge it
the edge of your foot   careful
as you watch its tumbling facets

Your hand stretches out   your fingers feel its texture
Yes   it will fit in the expanse of your hand
Your span   is wide enough
    its substance   solid enough
       your strength   sufficient
Now you grasp my idea   its cold solidity
    It's sharp enough to slice into your skin
       Do you see my point?

Look at where I'm going with this
The path stretches before us through luminous fields
into unfamiliar cities   & despite howling jackals
winds safely across the wilderness

Eventually it will lead to its logical conclusion
Do you follow me?

The Mona Lisa Speaks

Leonardo is obsessive   Can you imagine sitting here on
this painted poplar panel with one hand resting upon the other
motionlessly while he mixes & remixes paint on his palette   seeking
just the right intensity of colour for the flesh on the top side of my
wrist   the dimmed glow for my slightly shadowed   ringless fingers?
He's already used his quick skill to bring me to life   wasn't that
enough?   Why must he return   as days become years to scrape &
retouch what he's already done so well?   Why should I care if every
fold of my sleeve appears as though really seen   with glistening on
each top edge & darkened in between?   Why should I care if the misty
landscape of road   ridge   river & bridge has the sense of depth &
distance he hungers for?

Don't tell me of his love   He expects so much of me   expects me
to show the glory of his genius in the curve of my cheek   the subtle
curl of my lips   but couldn't he love me enough to let me be second
rate?   Even so   he makes me smile   I want to hold back   make him
wait & consider the intensity & depth of my staring eyes   & the veiled
darkness of my motionlessly falling hair

Continuously he gives the intolerable compliment of his attention

Forming a Line

Suppose I am writing a novel
    Through the wreck of a train
as a vehicle   so to speak   for plot development
I can solve several separate situations
I can   kill off one character   detain another
make a hero of my novel's hero (charging into the smoke
of a burning compartment)   & knock some sense
into yet another
all through the wreck of a train

Suppose you're a character in a novel I'm writing
or better yet   in a Shakespearean play   & yet
you're granted your say   concerning your part
(forgetting for now a writer's merciless intent)
or   instead   you're a wavy line
drawing yourself on a white sheet
You seek to synchronize with the greater whole
making sense   with the red lines I have predetermined
that   to you   seem to be forming left to right across the page
& with the other black lines (the other actors on the stage)
The red lines   are the props & propositions
around which you waltz   like a dancer choosing her steps
in relation to her partner's   & yet   I know your dance by heart
before you ever start   incorporating your black winding line
& the bent paths of others   into the art of my red ink design

Suppose Ophelia was developing her own voice
within Shakespeare's overall book   not knowing how Hamlet
or Laertes might respond   not knowing their lines
Was she drowned   sent down into the weeping brook
with her weedy trophies   because of the bard's choice
or because the branch broke?   There must have been room
(forgetting for now a writer directed her will)
for escape from her scripted doom
as with a real train thundering down the line

29

The Diver (The Grand Miracle)

If we look over his shoulder
as he looks into the depths   we see only
darkness   If we instead   view
him across the lake   every molecule will make
the striated sky & undulating streaks of water
draw our eyes   toward him
in a conspiracy of light & colour
Yet   if we held such a vantage point
we'd see him discard his garments
& without hesitation   plunge beneath the surface
his body losing its distinctness of hue
within the grey-green-blue of water
the image bending with the refracting light
until it vanishes in dark fathoms

His experience   a giving way of warmth
& murky light   as the lake grows darker & colder
as in the bleakest night   until black chill
surrounds him like death   & still
he descends   until his hands find the muddy bottom
The pressure presses upon his ears
& his lungs scream for breath
as he falls like a seed into a tomb   as though
entering a watery womb   like an unborn eagle
hidden within an egg in a dirty woven nest
like a worm drawn into a cocoon
Down among the slime & decay
he takes on the form of death
His final kicks   keep him within reach
as he scrounges down through the weeds
through the loose sand & soil
His fingers find the treasure he's sought   firmly grasping
it   lifting it   returning with it toward the surface

What we'd see   if we could be there
is the true colour returning to his shadowy shape
& a vision of what he's rescued   quite
different from its appearance deep in mud
Triumphantly he breaks into the air
lifting high his find   giving it a special place
water dripping from his arms
We'd watch as he rises again   like a lily bursting from its bulb
like a sun rising above the forested horizon
in full possession of the landscape   the water   & the light

PART THREE
What the Poet Sings

The Poet Weaves Three Worlds

Three worlds   the poet weaves
                (1)
The marvellous he believes
(though may not follow) which his boatswain
more suited for gallows   than pulpit
accepts as mysteries   directing an old man
to his knees
                (2)
The marvellous fictitious fantasies
of a magic book whose power swallows all
        in the tempest   & sends the sea's waves
        to ground the ship in shallows
        'round a desolate isle
of monster & spirit   enslaved for a while
        so that deities   perform for youths
of mythologies   all the more pliant
        because the poet disbelieves
                (3)
The world his eye perceives
whose histories   he also bends
into shadows of realities

The poet twists from these
a three-strand cord of truths

Something

Something amazing slips through
    in the way his guitar gently weeps
        a deep meaning that soon creeps
            well beyond his own comprehension
like what sings in the erratic swirl of a Van Gogh sky
    or more tangibly   Wordsworth's suspicion
        of what we'd glimpse if we were more in tune
            with the sea & the moon   The guitarist closes his eyes
& notes float   inevitably from vibrating strings
    Something out-flies the physics   a vision high above
        the skill of the musician   like the attraction that brings
            to beauty   obsessive claims of love

Some people   though   would trip over such a form
    wouldn't catch anything from an electric guitar
        like Jack Lewis whose tastes were of times long gone
            He would sip it from old world mysteries
drawn onward   like a ship through Nordic mist
    or Ulysses through the storm   drawn onward
        by tales of sirens sweetly singing
            as heard in his own mind   And what of us?
Will our grip slip as we seek to find   more
    of this cryptic joy   that drips upon various musics
        from a higher cup?   Might this cause us to look up
            with tongue and lip thirsting for more?

Mr Milton Tries to Read *The Philosopher's Stone*

For those who find the reading of footnotes
leaves them at the gates of Milton's paradise   lost
& twice as alone   imagine Milton   tossed
into a seventeenth century annotated edition
of *Harry Potter & the Philosopher's Stone*

Mr & Mrs Dursley of number four...
Since the advent of a general postal system (for delivering epistles
packages   & rejected poems) homes have posted a numerical
street address   on or beside the front door
Privet Drive...
In an odonym   Drive   is a synonym for Street   Road or Avenue
This particular designation arose with the increase of automobiles
(motorized vehicles with a combustion engine which spins their
wheels) which people are said to "drive"
were proud...
Pride has gradually shifted in meaning through the centuries
becoming a positive self image rather than one of the seven deadly
sins
to...

Here   Milton reaches the end of line one
& decides to read something simpler
such as George Herbert or John Donne

The Dark Clown

It is difficult not to feel that the entire war in heaven
is a huge practical joke to the Father . . .
—Northrop Frye

The Dark Clown tells his legion
　　freedom trumps submission
　　　　but once they join his insurrection
　　　　　he makes a revision
　　father of terrorism　vandalism
of that jolly greasepaint disguise
　　of the smiling frown
　　　　ism　deceiver　liar　boaster
　　　　　　faker　whose power-brag
　　　　　unwittingly salutes his maker
The Dark Clown　tries to rise higher
　　to aspire　to the sublime　& even he
　　　　sees irony　at creeping in the mouth
　　　　　of a sleeping snake
　　　　to mix with bestial slime
　　to miss what he was after
　　　　& be cast down to gnawing
　　　　　lake of fire　endure heaven's laughter
　　　　　　　& then to wake the hiss
　　　　　　& slither of hell's choir
　　　　　to cause such a fuss
　　　　then prove　ridiculous

Look at a Poem as You Would a Window

Look at a poem as you would a window
in the night   Rest your eyes on its reflective
sheen from within   With your interior bright
you'll see simply   a glass darkly
Now darken the house   cast your shadow across
your floor's moonlit parallelogram   & turn your eye
to spy heaven   & the face of the moon

Look at a poem as you would the moon
her pale light might easily
be swept from your room   but illuminates
enough for you to write your own poem
or to read this one by   From such a great height
her glory comes   Be enriched
but understand   it's second-hand

Look at a poem as you would the sun
to ponder what ignites such fire
& good work done in her light
even by one who sweeps a room
What matters is for whom   & how it's done
That's the alchemy   that transforms drudgery
all our lead turned to gold

On the Brink of Niagara

You & I have stood on the brink of Niagara many times
& so we know   like Coleridge   a waterfall can be sublime
   not merely pretty   & of all the waterfalls on earth
some are more majestic   more picturesque & grand   more worth
   the praise   more deserving of the description   We've worn
      raincoats
within reach of the descending water's spray   & on the boat
   Maid of the Mist   & kissed   as if to seal the event
Despite   the good   the true   the beautiful   some seem bent
   on destroying our ability to qualify such things
& deny the thundering   of which my soul sings

A Rabbit Tale

When Peter saw Mr McGregor wield
his hoe   in the middle distance
he saw also the extensive field
of onion   lettuce   & cabbage plants
to a little rabbit   mouth-watering for sheer size
& far beyond him   the white wooden gate
he must reach   to avoid his father's fate
of being baked into Mrs McGregor's pies

Peter had to deafen his ears   & harden
his heart to the only restriction his mother ever set
to run straight away to the forbidden garden
just to nibble stolen goods   but then he met
the gardener around the end of a cucumber frame
Mr McGregor   like the angel on Eden's east
prevented him from continuing his feast
flashing that hoe like a sword of flame

Lazarus to Stephen

Yes   I envy you
& have envied you for years
I've yearned
to face once more what we've both faced

Yes   I must go through
this life some more   My ears
listening for a chariot   not yet earned
spoiled for this life by that brief taste

Then   I never knew
that if returning   my fears
would be of living too long here   I've learned
sadly   an end can be erased

What then can I do?
Too slowly   my second death nears
Too eager   I'll never be stoned or burned
Too sad   my first death gone to waste

Yes   I'm the one to
reap in joy   followed by sowing in tears
for me it's backwards   it's turned
till I re-reach what I've now chased

In Search of Shakespeare

Prince Hamlet   with his book wondered if he
who made his character (& would make Lear)
the bard himself might be   or might not be
In castle rooms he longed to meet Shakespeare
Instead he met the queen & Claudius
& the whole plot he wanted to forget
with foolish questions came Polonius
oblivious to mocking by Hamlet
If face to face   he'd ask the famous writer
why dear Ophelia had to drown below
& why with swords he had to be a fighter
but you & I & everyone must know
if they're to meet some day   prolonged or fleeting
that Shakespeare must initiate the meeting

The World's Last Night

Lear's elder daughters
think they know how the story will end
to the point of plotting their father's death
to the point of plucking out Gloucester's eyes
But a nameless servant leaps to defend
him & dies despite a valiant fight

Regan's horrid shadowy shape rises
back-stab surprises him   his hour come round at last
Night falls   Patterns of betrayal repeat
Edmund thinks he'll defeat his brother
Goneril & Regan will eventually spend
their passionate intensity on each other

I remember a Korean turning & turning
driving 'round & 'round each bend
orbiting Queen's Park   megaphone proclaiming
precisely when the Second Coming
would be   Even then I sadly laughed
That date's now long passed

Lear doesn't know foe from friend
mad in the face of the storm's buffeting
His raging softens through suffering
with tears in his eyes for his youngest
Do we ever really know
how the play will end?

A Traveller in an Antique Land

He slips through the city gate with the fading light
starting his journey in the cool of night
when creepers   runners   & predators on the wing
populate the shadowy desert
Dark shapes shift in the hollows
swift figures cross the dunes
within sight of the rising moon

He won't walk the path of pilgrims
in the blazing days that follow   but the way
that seems right to him   Pans that clink
from dangle clips   tally each step of the trip
but not the cost   His water skins grow light
the sky oppressively bright   He finds he's lost
as he swallows his final sip

His lips are dry   the sun at its height
As many ways wind through the white sand
as there are steps that can be taken
He'd ignored   at the gate   what pilgrims say
of an oasis in this forsaken   shelterless land
Now it's too late   Boundless & bare
the lone & level sands stretch far away

No one saw him stop & stand   nor heard the clatter
when he stumbled   No one knows what lured
him across this land   Shifting sands
will have soon obscured where he fell
so no one can tell   he was ever there
Soon it won't matter   which wrong route he chose
across the wilderness   to miss the only well

Adoring

The song is sung for everyone
even the stiff-footed & thick-tongued
who've felt what the poet sings
& find the wings of these lines open a sky
where wordless hearts never fly
since the poet   far from instructing
simply brings to qualities & virtues   their due
& tunes strings to the true
for *the old poets*
such as Herbert   with Constancy
& Hopkins   with Pied Beauty
were not teaching but adoring

PART FOUR
Ready to Re-Ignite

The Humiliation

Like damp mist
freezing on a lamppost
this is the humiliation of myth into fact
the abstract   spilled like blood on concrete
the allusive grown bold
the ritual symbolic act   contracted
from everywhere   to the backside of nowhere
from mystery to history
from the always   down to these particular days

This names a town   a time   a governor
a man & his teen bride   Each lineage is traced
shows how the greatest humiliation took place
of God into Man
Here   the infinite condensed to infant
the eternal was confined   to one instant at a time

Nocturne with Monkey

We are inveterate poets
—C.S. Lewis

Does the capuchin monkey   hanging from his prehensile tail
see the stars   or just a speckled ceiling
beyond the Peruvian jungle's darkening canopy?
When his gathering of palm nuts is hindered
by the approach of creeping night
might he stop to consider those points of light?
Might he   staring into the deep
comprehend their distance
their size   their number   & then wonder
or is his imagination limited to foraging   & wedging
himself in high treetops for his night's sleep?
Might he be overcome with awe   or is the sight
of a shadowy snake or a slinking cat
at the foot of his tree   his only cause of fright?

A man   walking the terraces of night
might be preoccupied with inconsequential things
& not notice the   insufficiently bright
smudge of Andromeda's spiral
on a moonless night
but should he stop   to marvel at the sky's expanse
his considerations measure more than space & time
for numbers are only the foothold   from which
his imagination's leap   thrusts toward the sublime
Might it be his own shadow   the shadow of God's image
stretching across the galaxies   that carries such consequence
since merely seeing such blotches of light
seems to have no teeth   to bite a lesser mind?
We are left   like Pascal   terrified by the silence

Thrist

Thirst was made for water
  inquiry for truth

Raindrops were made for roots
roots were made for soil
soil   for life
            life   for glory

Raindrops were made for glory
listen   roof drumming
eaves dripping   look
glisten   sunlight catching
luminous liquid   inexpressible proof
  of something
    spoken by growling skies

Skies were made for glory
wings were made for skies
feathers   for wings
  among other things
    such as sheltering   & beauty
but mostly for the glory of soaring

Water was made for skies
& rain
        for trickle
                for gurgle
for rivulet   stream   creek & river
for puddle   pond   lake & ocean
for sip
        for swallow
for swim & sail
    submerge & drown
for hiding   inquiry   & eventual discovery
    a sparkling glass of truth

On a Summer's Day

As the stream gently flows   & her boat drifts
Beauty lets her fingers dangle   She knows
most minnows become lost   unable to follow
She lifts her head as in a dream   Her reflection
like a naiad   or the mirroring of the willow's daughter
ripples in the beam   shining over the ridge
across the water   Some who see   don't really see
yet she lingers   beneath the arching bridge
& lets her fingertips dip & drip   among the tangle
of reeds   where bright lilies float

She's spread herself down the meadowlands
& shed   her winter coat
although schoolboys   & farmhands
bumble by   dull to the joy they've killed
Still those really skilled   are meek enough
& seek enough   to not stand still
until they find   *Equality...has no place in the world*
of the mind   To those who scruff & scrape   & give
their all   Beauty's kind   Those who call & cry
after her   like after a rare bird   will be filled

When the guitarist tunes his strings
& uses up the bad notes in practice   Beauty floats
almost effortlessly   like a bird on the wing
settling comfortably on her perch
She laughs at democracy   being most heard
under ripe conditions
She will sing with musicians   who kiss the sky
& whisper her word to pilgrims
whose search   leads them to compare Monet
to real waterlilies on a summer's day

About the Feeder

Drawn on by the sparseness of winter
feathers flutter about the feeder

The woodpecker pecks with no sound
& peppers   on the snow   scattered seed

Chickadees flit in   but don't stay
pick some small morsel & fly away

They chatter at each other   but sing
for us   their recognizable song

With barely the patience to not move
I once fed a sparrow on my glove

Might the mutual love still remain
between timid songbirds & man?

The Abolition of Man

He stands with a book in his hands and sees through
   his glasses   believing he sees through
      the arguments of the author he reads
         It's one thing to see through a disguise
quite another to see through a face

The man in tweed laughs
   Loyalty is a hedging of bets
      discipline   the practical side of greed
         love   the hunger for a need
He can see through anything

She raises a marble obelisk   speaks of dignity
   & grace   He makes a crack   plants his seed
      explains how atoms race   through empty space
         & then explains the atoms away
She leaves with nothing in her hand

What is most important   he would say   *is to understand*
   If knowledge becomes the new commodity
      worth more than human life   will he harden
         his head   or see through his sawing
of the limb beneath our feet

He walks to the wall   where he sees
   through his glasses   & through the window
      to see the garden & the street
         But if he sees through the garden
& the street   he sees nothing at all

Moon Landing

She settles in the clouds like a bird on her nest
draws our eyes   like a debutante's smile

Like competing suitors at a Victorian ball
two prospective partners   each
circle closer   but one first takes the chance
reaches his hand   makes one small step
one giant leap   & touches her   desiring to dance

She turns to stone

Through the darkness we watch the moon fly
Nothing's changed
She's aloof   & that real journey
across the dance floor of the sky   cannot satisfy
the impulse   space travel tales gratify

That distant girl's face   & her form   is traced
in moonlight across the terrace   more beautiful
than any girl could be   her wild hair
sways as though in the wind   her shadow
engulfs the universe

She slips through the clouds like a ship through mist
draws our imaginations higher

Since those who've reached with measuring rods
have lost their desire   we reach
only with our eyes   our mouths agape
so our fire of fascination
will still burn   as she rises over rooftops

Life on Other Planets

A curious boy's science   dreams
of crop circles   sky saucers   of planets
populated by insect-men   whose transporter   beams
them through light streams   beyond the moon
A man's nervous nightmare   screams of invasion
from a remote & unknown star   where knowledge far
exceeds our own   fears   beings of evil intent
without form   & morally void   being sent here
Then there's the astronomer bent
on disproving God's existence
by discovering life is not peculiar
to our planet   or by displaying that it is
Distances beyond earth's atmosphere
boggle the boy's brain   calculating time
moving at light speed   How long to reach   near
or distant stars?
What if aliens could easily span
the galactic gap   timelessly   but consider
the vastness of space   insulation
between themselves   & our bent race?

Flamboyance

The wild rose   summer's flower
along the fading path grows sweet
though it only lives & dies to itself
& spring's unseen trilliums   in forest shade
are lost   only to us   if the haste
of our lives won't let us pass
Such flamboyance draws things
on delicate wings   & never goes to waste
though like grass   soon withering

The scientist   in lab coat or hip-waders
knows   to seek meaning in what he observes
The poet suspects   the right metaphors
await her   astir in stream glisten
                afloat in pond stillness
                asleep in forest glade
for *nature makes nothing in vain*
Colour & camouflage   ash & flame
seem ready to re-ignite   as we listen

In the Shelterless Street

Wind whispers rumours of rain
a threat of recurring wet   we never
want to claw   in the shelterless street
be seen soaked to the skin
outside all those closed doors

Rain won't wash grime's relentless cling
from hands rubbed raw
wash gutters clean   end exile
or clear clutter from our brains
Its drum on wet wood won't get us in

Handles shake   shoulders batter to force locks
but there's no answer to our knocks
Wind scatters leaves from trees
rustles leaves in the book that assures us
we need not   be shut out   forever

Wind whispers of what matters
pushes rainclouds away
All our lives we yearn to behold
& be held   to no longer hide
to see every door open   & be drawn inside

To Know

One of the things that distinguishes man from the other animals is that he wants to know things, wants to find out what reality is like, simply for the sake of knowing.

−C.S. Lewis "Man or Rabbit?"

Once you know   what you know
you can't unknow it   not once you've figured it out
Once you have reason to believe
you can't honestly cling to doubt
though you may simply want to go
along your merry way
That would be like the man who receives
a letter & suspects the bank's foreclosing or   say
a loved one has taken a turn for the worse
Has he gained anything real
preserved his precarious wealth
or maintained his relative's health
by not breaking the envelope's seal?
If you don't know   you don't know
like a woman unaware of a thief's hand in her purse
but when we choose to look the other way
it simply isn't so

Passage

Mary sets down her work
the author sets down his pen
Mary doesn't wait for him to pick it up again
frozen in her own time   like actors in tableau
unaware of any delay
Her author   unhurried by the pace of her day
lives beyond his novel   although
well aware of the pause

The sun stood still over Gibeon
the moon   motionless   over the valley all day
to the dismay of five invading kings

Unheard footfalls   already written
echo down an untaken passage
towards an unopened door
into the rose garden
The author's not bound   by sequence
story-time or what has gone before
Mary sets down her work   & immediately
a knock comes at the door

Piano Lesson

If you hit the right keys at the right time   the instrument plays itself
J.S. Bach once said   which I find true   Every time I play the Goldberg
Variations   on the stereo   Glenn Gould's piano plays flawlessly

A good pianist makes her mistakes at rehearsal   not altering mid-
phrase as the groomsmen gather at the altar   nor as an impediment
to the soloist   preparing to sing   It's a matter of timing

The surprise with pianos   is there are no wrong keys
C.S. Lewis has noted   Every single note is right
at one time   & wrong at another

When I took lessons   I admit I struck good keys badly
untimely   a pedestrian standing at a green light
wearing sandals in the snow

There are 360 possible degrees to lean   away from perpendicular
eighty-seven keys other than the right one   although a jazz musician
might find an alternative   if the timing's right

But if your timing is as off as a photographer's
who falls in love with the bride   or one who opens the shutter
when the bridesmaids turn aside   it's not a good picture

Good is not good   when it goes off course   a luxury liner
colliding with an iceberg   a dissonant note in a major chord
or the marriage of true minds   with selfish hearts

We all know good may go bad   lilies can fester
at the front of the church   the pianist's cell phone might chirrup
as the couple strains for *I do*

Democracy

What could be more equalizing than a grocery line?
No matter your income or education
you still have to wait   for the elephantine matron to debate
the price of twinkies with the cashier-in-training
So you scan the magazines   The revelation
of an actress gaining forty inexplicable pounds   leaps
from a headline   The latest swimsuit issue
will mess with your head   unless you avert your eyes
A voice calls for a cleanup in aisle eight   thunders
a special on toilet tissue   The latest diet sensation in the rack
promises wonders   You stack veggies & bread
on the conveyor belt   hope your ice cream won't melt
as the same woman recounts her change   Once in every generation
the paparazzi snap a royal honeymoon vacation   Once a week
some Hollywood couple gets divorced   Why do we emulate
the famous   even those who by choice make their lives disasters?
Who longs for equality   who deserves power?   Aristotle
said some people are only fit to be slaves   C.S. Lewis questioned
if any are fit to be masters

After Evensong

In defeat we sink   *through the deathlike hours*
like stones descend to the lakebed
despite our desire   like sparks that fly upward
eventually settling to the ground   like
the dust we shall return to   or a windless kite

Like cranky toddlers   we can only fight
so long   not strong enough to stay vertical
or resist rubbing our eyes
although   wise men know darkness is deep
& in the end   the dark is right

For soon we all are ravished by sleep
helpless to defend our ravaged wills
from our bodily need   In such a river
much pleasure must flow
it buoys us   on its current all night

Even those at close of day   who do not pray
the Lord   their souls to keep
must give in   perchance to dream
of sky-high leaps   or deep ocean dives
both shimmering in radiant light

The one who never slumbers   lifts us
on the hull of his song   lulls us
along the willowy stream
& onto the swelling tide
& safely drifts us   within his sight

Waiting

A man & woman wait by a window
for a third who's overdue
The sky reddened with evening
as the hour of his arrival approached
& then passed   *Your friend's not coming*
she says   *He is coming* her husband replies
despite the hollow halo of the streetlight
for he's been promised
The evidence of the dark street   an hour later
& the clock's progressive testimony   are proof
enough for her   She turns away
How will the husband feel if he turns
off the porch light   just before his friend arrives
hat in hand   apologetic for the unavoidable delay?
He waits   with proof of a different kind

Truth in Myth

When Balder   god of summer   died
tears that his goddess mother cried
fell as the fruit of mistletoe
He rose   returning to her side

Adonis   had no way to know
a vicious boar would lay him low
Zeus brings him back for half the year
but he lies dead with winter snow

Osiris   was to Isis dear
but killed   so conquering her fear
she sang a song as one divine
rejuvenation in his ear

The Roman   Bacchus   god of wine
reborn each spring   to us a sign
We turn to winter a brave face
because new life is in the vine

The myths like these in every race
hint of what did   & does   take place
for resurrection once   by grace
occurred in history   time & space

On the Latest Impending Doom

So   you've found a new engine of doom
running on fossil fuel   to drive us to despair
Like horses that have fled a hollow roar
run wide-eyed through fields
& then been led back to the shed   we're insecure
with blind fear of claws   teeth or enveloping fire
that can burn a barn to cinders   turn the air
to charred memory in stallion nostrils' snort & flare
Who needs new science to kindle dread
whether coastal cities be flooded or simply left behind?
Yes   we should care   & dare to shoulder what we can
but if we blindly believe either extreme
both fears & hopes are swindlers   No new dangers
make angels fear to tread   since time won't always be
The good in life may seem to dwindle if our focus
is the uncertain road ahead   instead
glimpse the happy orchards   on either side
After one short sleep we wake eternally

PART FIVE
With New Eyes

The Great Divorce

None of us believed it would go well when we received
the invitation   How could our darling   Heaven
concede to marry Hell?
Despite Blake's best intention   it began with inferences of fighting
& ended with Hell citing   irreconcilable differences

The sky was bleak   & drained greyness into the streets
in the form of drizzling rain   yet grew no brighter
Walking through the suffering city   I turned the thermostat
down on Dante's inflammatory images
I found   no errant popes buried head-first
bare feet burning in the air   no one at all
just dreary tenements   & abandoned warehouses
empty freight yards   & neglected shops
I walked on   my coat getting wetter
the stained twilight never altered   & if this was
the bad side of town   I never saw anything better

Finally people   just this side of night   forming a miserable line
down at the bus station   I joined the queue
& waited for the first bus leaving town   Such bickering
made me wonder how they could stand   on the same street

Imagine   much later   disembarking where the air is bright
& the foliage richly green   where we   the grim travellers
seem transparent smudges   against sky & trees
grey ghosts   unable to bend grass   beneath insubstantial feet
the landscape   more expansive
than our closed-in little solar system
the grass   solider than on earth

Travellers with a knack for finding trouble in paradise
cling to the known
old men refuse a doctor's advice
horses run back to the burning barn
They turn to board the bus   returning   safely   to the grey

Wisdom from Malacandra

(A glimpse into the space trilogy of C.S. Lewis)

Imagine landing on a slighter planet
one less stressed by its own mass
a world unbent by war in the heavens
unsuppressed by corruption
one with lighter elongated landforms
its plant life   reaching like precarious trees
its beings   long & slender

At first you'll see nothing clearly
until you know enough   to know
what you're looking at
to interpret an unmoving purple mass
on the far shore   as mountain
or cloud   or something growing

Gradually your eyes will adjust
but you'll also see our heavier world
with new eyes   notice the known twist
against this new plumbline   discover
why ours is called the silent planet

The fastest thing our senses perceive
is light   although it is not the light we see
but slower things illuminated by it
The faster something moves   the closer it is
to being in two places at once
If it is faster still   the moving thing
will be in all places at once
It will be so fast that it is at rest
Such are the *eldila*

They will not speak to us of size or number
for these merely confuse us   so that
we reverence trifles   & pass by the truly great

Even the *hrossa* know   a pleasure is full grown
only when it is remembered

Innocence of Perelandra

(Another glimpse into the space trilogy of C.S. Lewis)

Imagine awakening on a floating island
where the landscape rolls with the waves
undulates with their will
like a flick rolling along a rope
making it hard to stand   harder to walk
in the way you're accustomed

I was young yesterday   the green lady tells you
for it had never occurred to her to hope
for something other   to wish the wash of waves
Maleldil sends   will cease
or to desire a good   other than what's in sight
or on its way
She's not mastered our ability to make
the fruit we find   insipid
by focussing the mind
on what we'd anticipated

It occurs to you   suddenly   that her purity & peace
are fragile   not that they'll inevitably crumble
but simply that they might

The Somnambulist

(The Deputy Director in That Hideous Strength)

The somnambulist floats from room to room
humming a tune   His shoes creak
as he passes through passages
& vaguely looks towards those
who'd least like to have him overhear their words
Their conversation   afterwards   does not resume

He looks across his wide desk as from a great distance
& rambles indistinctly of imprecise abstractions
He turns his unfocussed eyes toward the ceiling
& passively mumbles directives to *show no lack of initiative*
but to *not exceed authorized actions*
before he succumbs to other distractions

The somnambulist floats from room to room
untroubled by troublesome knowledge
even by the imminence of his ruin
for he's ceased to believe in knowledge itself
Nothing can be done   to waken him to reality
for he's convinced there is none

He slips from danger in the dining room
yet a fatal lethargy prevents his further escape
Instead his stooped figure can be seen
as he passes through passages
creaking   pacing   humming a tune
proceeding to the place of his final doom

What Lucy Saw

On the day after the night on which she woke
& wandered through pools of moonlight
& spoke   to the trees   a whispered invitation
almost an incantation   to also waken
that made them rustle in the windless air
& to almost heed her
the children became lost in an unfamiliar wood

It was then she saw him   between
two mountain ashes   before he vanished
like some evanescent vapour
a great lion   *The* great Lion
his mane outshining the sun
there   then not there   where he'd been
unseen by the others   leaving her verity
unverifiable   unbelievable
though believed   by one who'd not seen
who later received   his *well done*

A Parliament of Owls

(a fantasy)

In the hush of night   with the rush of wings
an owl bears you   to where you
witness rare & whispered things
      tu-whoo   tu-whoo
His flight alights on the edge of a ledge
of a once-arched window
within the ivy-covered bower
of a crumbling tower   engulfed in shadow
In the cooing dark you hear a flutter
of feathers   a whir of hurry & flurry
in the air   & wonder   in the mutter
      tu-whoo   tu-whoo
if they worry whether   they dare share
the secrets of the fowls
in this parliament of owls   with such as you
But as with whoosh & thrust he flew
you knew nothing   but trusted he was true
As your eyes adjust   through the gloom
you're aware   they would rather gather
in this towered room   to compare points of view
      tu-whoo   tu-whoo
than do what they could do

Contemplation

You trudge dirt roads   a pilgrim of your heart's desire
till your blistered feet tire
At the House of Wisdom you crawl to bed
where woods lie lovely   dark & deep
& soon you're asleep

When you wake in the night   a full moon   large & low
shines in at your window
& a woman   standing there   lifts her hand
to keep the silence unbroken
for you'd have spoken

Out to the grassy lawn   she leads you by moonlight
to forests of the night
She instructs you to leap the deep crevice
You fly high over pines   non-stop
to the mountain top

Her name is Contemplation   grey Wisdom's daughter
Out across the water
she shows you the island of your desire
You consider it by moonlight
as from a great height

The Shove & Tumble

from the perspective of the demon Screwtape

If you've allowed him to grow humble
when he fumbles   hint he should be proud
of his humility   Like a shadow examined under
bright light   it will have died   Praise him
so he stumbles on the pride of beating his pride

Our game's loud rumbles hide   the wide
world's concerns   & turn his eyes to futility
     humility-boasts   & mumble-shame

If a man knew he had great ability
(a gift of grace)   he could be humble
& not even know it if he shoved the idea aside
If he shoved the idea aside   he could be a poet
if unafraid to tumble   into mystery's embrace

Among the Tombs

In the desert after nightfall
each sound seems louder
each stark tomb   larger

Their gaping   hollow mouths
exhale darkness
into the darkness

You follow the large   silent cat
whose eyes glint in the moonlight
& hint of inaccessible secrets

He stares northward across desert sand
while you place your back to his
eyeing your fear

Conspicuously absent
are the companions   supposed
to meet you here

So much of what you understand
is not what is   like the strange dreams
you fall into   with your sleep

Aping Presence

The ape enacted a fraud   on the edge of a clearing
tricks in the half-light of a bonfire   nearing
the edge of night   a con upon those hungry for hope
traps set with scraps of fact   stirred
into their desire   so they saw & heard
what they wanted to see
Playing God   with a coat of skin & rope
he was almost caught   about to be found out
but ruthlessly cast the doubt   back on reality
the knot pulled tight around truth's throat

PART SIX
Playful Pulse

Psalm of Incarnation

Every born fish submits to its
　　submerged swim   every beast
　　　　& bird to walk & wing

Every sparrow & swallow will sing
　　will be heard   fine-tuned men
　　　　& angels will raise a voice

People take pleasure in the playful pulse
　　of words   & the Word participated
　　　　in the joy of words well-stated

Poetry is an incarnation
　　an embodiment of what has previously been
　　　　unheard & unseen

The Death of Words

Devils are unmaking language
Reprehensible   revolting   ruiners   run nouns into the ground
Cruel   cold   contemptible connivers   drive verbs to the edge of town
until they cough & chug to a standstill with the needle far below E
& leave them to the casual neglect   every wreck receives
that eats them down to the dust   like rust
& leaks their meaning into the soil   like oil
Destructive   diabolical swine   won't cast pearls
but the words they hurl   in a diatribe   as terms of abuse
dashed down   slash their own precision   like air
from their tires   & sabotage the spare
until descriptions no longer describe
Foul   detestable   deplorable   despicable devils
rip consonants from vowels
lift the hood on smart little adverbs
to force disconnections   & slice their wires
set fires in their backseats
so participles clash   conjunctions crash
poison pollutes their particularity
& those vile villains smash their identities with misuse
which creeps   like those insidious spider-like lines
in a windshield   growing from chip   to asterisk
to become a crack so wide   it cannot hide
until the sledgehammer comes down
to obliterate every distinction

Winterlake

projected from a line by C.S. Lewis

The hunter wind & the hound frost
have lost their way   snow blind
I feel the icy hands clasped
but losing grip   I see the expanse
of frozen lake   stretching
from the distant narrows
to where the pines' outline
blurs in the whirling flakes
Shadows overtake the brightness
& the whiteness fills the shadows

In the morning stillness
tracks dent the horizontal sheet
& whisper   *follow   follow*

The Silence of One Voice

When we shake our fists at God   & relish despair
the silence of one voice beats like waves
that wash from us who have not   even what we have
swish sand   from the sand   from the sand
so all we have to build on are the pulsing echoes
of our anger   that anaesthetic of the mind
that dismisses every reasonable sound
every hint of solid ground   like how the susurration
of rain   or the hiss of tire-spin on the wet street   drowns
what we'd otherwise hear   or how the barrier of a sand dune
or thick summer leaves will absorb distant sound
Trying to call the tune   we beat our heads
against the silence   like a trapped bee expecting to pass
out to open fields through solid glass

Undergrowth

To travel the woods of language
we care   too often   only of general direction
shrug   at never arriving
choose a trail   so worn it can only lead
to someone else's conclusion
& wander into inherited phrases
whose original meanings we can only guess
like the path we walk near Limehouse
which was probably once a lane   if not a road
where the remnants of two ditched cars
have now deteriorated beyond recognition
   The thoughts of many slip   like wheels into a rut
to circumlocute the meaning even from themselves
They walk the talk   but without conviction
like a politician's borrowed speech
or the vain repetition of an unembraced liturgy
   The Wind moves   over the face
of the water   & over the land   as trees recede
& bow their heads   & rocks tremble
   We bumble through the undergrowth
of language   say what we only partially mean
stumble over simple similes   tumble over hard sayings
& if taken literally   blaspheme   Lord   in your *great*
unbroken speech   our limping metaphor translate

PART SEVEN
Sailing Through Mist

The Atlantic

I remember dissecting the dark mysteries of theology
one night   on a Florida beach in my youth
the Atlantic breathing as though alive
 my friends & I having followed
 the red ribbon of I-75
 all the way from Detroit to the coast
It was as though   by our free will   we were predestined
to oversimplify the vastness we faced
to participate in the cartography of the Holy Ghost
 experiencing the salty taste
 the wind stirring high in the palm trees
 & the joy of the shore   as our strength
Essential   though like a futile attempt to embrace
the sea   to put that entire ocean in a bottle
to be slipped into a message

Tumbled by the Surf

The first time I plunged into the Atlantic
    it wasn't really swimming the breakers curled
      like the sweeping waves on Lake Huron
    but higher longer stronger
more glorious able to lift & carry me
    if I submitted to their way with a rush push
      swirl & whoosh all around my ears
    & the forgotten tang of salt on my lips
To keep both feet planted in the sand
    where waves drew back then washed
      shells & pebbles higher up the strand
    or one foot or even a toe on the bottom
was like a chain The freedom of floating
    like a kite on the wind only came
      when I gave in

Apologetics

When you start to doubt if you exist
God believes in you

−Pierce Pettis

I am because I think   Descarte declared
& so   perhaps some people aren't   (or barely)
I mourn the slow disappearance of others
my parents   both in their nineties
their lives shrinking   silty white patches motionless beneath the trees
Reality settles in shadows   a bare twig snaps underfoot
One misstep & we misunderstand
though one day all will come clear

Professor Lewis had Professor Kirke profess
just three options   truth   lies   or madness
but sometimes we're mistaken   or misunderstood
& besides   who gets half   of what the parables say?
Sometimes we just have to close our eyes
& step out of the boat   look along the shimmer-path
& follow   across wave & trough
never mind   what we think we can prove

Does the cat chase her tail when she sees it move
or does it move   when she tries to catch it?
Aristotle   perhaps the prime prover
to suggest a prime mover   goes deeper than chickens & eggs
As I try to convince the flightless they too can fly
despite the illogical leap from nest into midair   I stand
under more than I understand   I sit under shade
that defies comprehension   & try not to lie

Lion

On a moonless night   whether
comprehended   or not   the tawny shine
of his mane sends forth its own light

He moves where he chooses   untamed
by our wishes   At the moment you anticipate
he comes   or delays

He comes   when desired most
or once hope has slipped
through your fingers   through the grate

His soundless approach   weakens muscles
lifts spirits   stammers perception
crumples certainty

Unpredictably there   though always there
the lion listens   illumines the hillside
suddenly seen   & then not seen

The compulsion that is his eyes
looks   & then turns away
expects you to follow

On a moonless night   the great lion
moves through swaying grass
bathed in moonlight

Ghost Ship

It was never intended like that
nailing clouds to the sky
Instead   it's the shape of a ghost ship
sailing through mist   waves against our prow
as hushed as sounds in a distant dream
The wind must blow where it will
Our blind fingers grope
we seek the tangible in spite of ourselves
tend to trust unworthy lifeboats   tradition
or the sailor's manual   both beautiful
in their own way   but leaky as hell
& never intended for this

Let wind push hair in your face
let flames alight on your brow
like Saint Elmo's fire high on the mast
though for now   you can't see the bow
for thick fog   ephemeral enough
to make you doubt everything
Relax   though decks slope & ropes sting
this ship's truly unsinkable
our captain dependable   though unseen
despite how we've messed with mystery
Remember those who've already made the crossing
that great cloud of witnesses

Wick

The night is dark & cold   Hope
is the spark that's caught hold of me

for I am the wick within the lantern
of the body   & I yearn to burn with light

My thirst is first to fill with oil
but then to ignite   to illuminate

white lace & polished things   to fling
bright gold about the room

to participate in the glory   & to spill
out into the night   I desire

to claim the morning star
to expire in the splendour of the fire

to be consumed
& be one with the flame

The Vocation of Maples

Might maples sense purpose beyond themselves
shade makers   wind breakers
nest bearers   leaf sharers   might roots
hold the hillside with a vocation of stabilization?

Stem tips let go   leaves twirl down
whirl to the ground   & eventually enrich earth
Might these trees thirst   or merely send
passionless roots to fetch water?

Might they strive for sun   or coolly bend branches
& stretch leaves into every gap?
Might maples long to unfurl in green beauty
& for sap to run   or merely take whatever comes?

If they freely submit dry limbs for the fire
might they approach their roles with the joint
sensations of duty & desire   as we do
in response to that scarcely heard voice?

Plastic Flute

      If a two-dimensional man could bound
from the canvas   on which the artist's painted him
a sower abandoning sunlit fields
a lover leaving his two-dimensional wife alone
in *Starry night over the Rhône*
would he not be astounded
by the way real lights glisten across real water
by the way grain waves in the wind
& far-away-forests gradually grow
in size & detail as you approach?
What in his experience could prepare him?
      If you were to play on a plastic flute
a Vivaldi concerto for lute   strings & harpsichord
for a gathering of primitives who've never heard
anything close   could you convey the sensation
of such an ensemble?   Could they rightly show you
they know what you mean?
      If you were to point to something
for a dog who doesn't know you   might he not
just sniff at your finger   focus on the fact
but miss the meaning?
      If you were given bread & wine
might you taste something more on your tongue?
      If you were to unfurl the blueprints
might you clearly comprehend a city
with twelve gates   each made from a gigantic pearl?

Signature

The signature of each soul
has its own curves & curls   its own loops & tails
Pick up your pen to trace yours
You'd think you'd know instinctively
but your hand can't quite form
the secret name imprinted upon your being
& on the white stone pendant   you'll be given

The shape of each soul
is a key   worn around your neck
impressed on your heart's tablet
uniquely formed to fit one lock   in one door
in a many-roomed mansion   Your well-suited suite
even has the music   your ears have always been
preparing for   already playing

The song of each soul
has its own time signature   its own voice
Each finger fits only the whorl
left by its own intimate touch
each key   its own door
& yet we all find each other
in the one awaiting us

Destination

A five-hour walk   a twenty-minute drive
the shortest distance   as the crow flies

If time is a straight line   God is the whole page
the landscape through which the road goes

the floodplain through which the river flows
the mountains   & the distant age

when they rose   & when the last star dies
in a conspiracy of light   a home to arrive

Notes & Acknowledgements

I want to thank those who have been an encouragement to me throughout the writing of this book: Christian Amondson, Brad Davis, Bill Fledderus, Brett Foster, John & Marion Franklin (Imago), Richard Greene, Malcolm Guite, Dave Harrity, David Kent & Margo Swiss, Luci Shaw, Karen Stiller, John Terpstra, The Rabbit Room, The Word Guild, The League of Canadian Poets, and the family I love so deeply and am so proud of. Appreciation goes to the delightful group of writers who often meet in our home (my own Inklings) and who had the first kick at many of these poems. Brett Foster and Richard Greene both spent considerable time and effort assisting with this collection's editing. Thank you.

"Of This & Other Worlds"—is a poem inspired (of course) by the C.S. Lewis essay "Of This & Other Worlds"—which is in the book *Of This & Other Worlds* (1992, Collins)—and by the first Narnia novel: *The Lion, the Witch and the Wardrobe*.

"The Longing"—comes from the material in chapter one, "The First Years" of *Surprised by Joy*, Lewis's autobiography—particularly starting at page 12 in my old Fontana paperback; by page nineteen, Lewis says of this longing (which he identifies with the German word Sehnsucht), "It had taken only a moment of time; and in a certain sense everything else that had ever happened to me was insignificant in comparison." This poem was first published in *Time of Singing*.

"Proof"—is built backwards from a idea in Lewis's finest novel, *Till We Have Faces*. (In my old Fount paperback it's page 135, which is in chapter XI.) It also uses material from *Surprised by Joy* and other biographies, including Alan Jacobs's excellent book, *The Narnian* (2005, Harper San Francisco).

"Silent Walks"—starts with a quote from *Surpised by Joy* (p. 115) and draws on information found in *The Narnian* (p. 53–4), and from *The Inklings of Oxford* by Harry Lee Poe and James Ray Veneman (Zondervan, p. 86ff). Warnie is Lewis's brother. The poem also references Tolkien's *The Fellowship of the Ring* (Unwin), and Lewis's *Out of the Silent Planet* (Scribner). This poem was first published in *The Lamp-Post*.

"Broadcast Talks"—was the original title of the material that eventually became *Mere Christianity*. You can listen to some surviving recordings (as I have) on YouTube. The sound of his voice, described in my poem as his *hoom tum toom*, comes from J.R.R. Tolkien's Ent, Treebeard, whose voice is said to have been inspired by the sound of Lewis's voice when lecturing or debating. This poem was first published in *Ruminate*.

"Oxford Downpour"—relates to our experience, when my wife and I visited the Oxford pub, famously frequented by Lewis and the Inklings, "The Eagle & Child" (a.k.a. "The Bird & Baby"). This poem was first published in *Third Way*.

"Magdalen College" "—was written with the creative assistance of Humphrey Carpenter's descriptions (p. 128–29, and 197–98) from his book *The Inklings* (Unwin Paperbacks, 1981) of Lewis's rooms at Magdalen College, Oxford, and what took place at Thursday night meetings.

"Hedonics"—is the title of a journalistic essay from the Harcourt collection *Present Concerns* (1986). The epigraph is a line from the opening paragraph of the essay.

"An Aversion to Film"—begins with a quote from the Lewis essay "On Stories" (which can be found in *Of This & Other Worlds*, p. 41). The book and film first referred to is *King Solomon's Mines* by Rider Haggard. The question closing the poem relates to the disappointing movie version of *Prince Caspian*. From childhood on, C.S. Lewis was known as Jack. To see his comments on the dwarfs in Disney, see *A Preface to Paradise Lost* (p. 58, Oxford University Press). This poem was first published in *Windhover*.

"Surprised By Joy"—has nothing to do with the Lewis autobiography of this name, except the obvious play on words. The material is available in various biographies, including Alan Jacobs's, *The Narnian* (p. 267ff). Jack married Joy Davidman Gresham in a civil ceremony on April 23, 1956.

"Grief Observed"—partially comes from the metaphors Lewis uses, particularly in section IV (page 68ff of my yellowing Bantam Books edition) of *A Grief Observed*.

"Extrapolations"—is about what Lewis was seeking to get at in *The Four Loves* (around page 115 in my Fontana paperback edition) in the chapter entitled "Charity." This poem was first published in *The Other Journal*.

"The Sacred Fish"—are the last three words of chapter XI "Scripture" in *Reflections on the Psalms* (page 100 in my Fontana paperback). Like several in this collection, this poem grows from extending Lewis's metaphor. This poem was first published in *Sojourners*.

"Bottle"—comes from the same chapter in *Reflections on the Psalms*. The italicized words in the poem are quoted from page 95 in my copy.

"The Coinage of your Brain"—leaps out of the C.S. Lewis poem "The Apologist's Evening Prayer" (found in the Harcourt collection *Poems*). The title alludes to *Hamlet*.

"The Possibilites"—originated from chapter five of *The Lion, the Witch and the Wardrobe* (on page 50 of my hardcover HarperCollins edition). This poem was first published in *Windhover*.

"If A Poet"—is my extension of one of Lewis's ideas from his essay "The Seeing Eye." The specific image is on page 171 from the Eerdmans collection *Christian Reflections*.

"Canine Inquiry"—is my extension of another of Lewis's analogies. It can be found on page 165 of *Christian Reflections* in an address called "Modern Theology and Biblical Criticism"; the same essay is in the Fontana collection *Fern-seed and Elephants* and was renamed by Walter Hooper as the title piece for that book.

"The Dogs"—originated from a comment in the first paragraph of chapter XI in *Letters To Malcolm* (page 60 in the Fontana paperback). This poem was first published in *Relief*.

"Metaphor"—begins with a quote from chapter X, "Horrid Red Things" of *Miracles* (page 76), and came from ideas in that chapter.

"The Mona Lisa Speaks"—is my expansion of what Lewis says in *The Problem of Pain* (page 30 in my Fontana edition) from the chapter called "Divine Goodness."

"Forming A Line"—comes from another Lewis analogy; this time it's from *Miracles*, "Appendix B On 'Special Providences'" (p.179ff of my well-used Fontana edition). This poem was first published in *Convivium*.

"The Diver"—is another expansion of a Lewis metaphor. This is from chapter XIV "The Grand Miracle" from *Miracles* (p. 115ff).

"The Poet Weaves Three Worlds"—comes from what Lewis says in the second chapter "Allegory" of his 1936 literary study *The Allegory of Love* (Oxford University Press—p. 82). The boatswain, and so on, are from *The Tempest*.

"Something"—comes from an illustration Lewis used in a footnote—concerning the term Sehnsucht which he calls "spilled religion"—in the essay "Christianity And Culture" in *Christian Reflections* (p. 23). My allusions are to the Wordsworth poem "The World is Too Much With Us; Late and Soon", and to songs by George Harrison, and Cream.

"Mr Milton Tries to Read *The Philosopher's Stone*"—plays with a comment (on page 62) in *A Preface to Paradise Lost; (*see also page 56). The italicized words, when put all together, form the opening line of J.K. Rowling's novel *Harry Potter and the Philosopher's Stone* (at least in my Raincoast edition).

"The Dark Clown"—also comes from an idea expressed in *A Preface to Paradise Lost* (p. 95).

"Look at a Poem as You Would a Window"—is another poem that comes from "Christianity And Culture" in *Christian Reflections* (p. 24). The George Herbert poem "The Elixir" is referenced in both the essay and my poem.

"On the Brink of Niagara"—originated from the opening page of Lewis's little book *The Abolition of Man*; the chapter is called "Men Without Chests" (and begins of page 7 of the Fontana edition). This poem was first published in *Perspectives*.

"A Rabbit Tale"—refers to characters and situations in Beatrix Potter's *The Tale of Peter Rabbit*, and particularly to the picture on page 48 (Frederick Warne & Co). Lewis was enamored with her stories as a child, and makes a point using this story in *A Preface to Paradise Lost* (p. 72)—which I expand. This poem was first published in *Saint Katherine Review*.

"Lazarus To Stephen"—is my flip of the Lewis poem "Stephen To Lazarus" from *Poems*. He wrote something similar in a letter on 25 June 1963: "How awful it must have been for poor Lazarus who had actually died, got it all over, and then was brought back . . ." It's in *Letters To An American Lady* (Eerdmans, p. 119). This poem was first published in *Crux*.

"In Search of Shakespeare"—expands an analogy in *Surprised by Joy*—chapter XIV "Checkmate" (p. 181). This poem was first published in *Windhover*.

"The World's Last Night"—is the title of a paper in *Fern-seeds and Elephants* (p. 76). The poem expands Lewis's analogy. Queen's Park is in Toronto, where the Ontario provincial parliament sits. This poem was first published in *Sehnsucht*.

"A Traveller in an Antique Land"—alludes to Shelley's sonnet "Ozymandius." My poem's origins are in a comment by Lewis in the sermon "A Slip of the Tongue," which appears in *Screwtape Proposes a Toast: and other pieces* (Fountain Books, p. 125).

"Adoring"—comes from the first page of the opening dedication (to Charles Williams!) in *A Preface to Paradise Lost*. The italicized words in my poem are Lewis's.

"The Humiliation"—is based on Lewis's words in "Is Theology Poetry" from *Screwtape Proposes a Toast: and other pieces* (p. 51). Again, the italicized words in my poem are Lewis's. This poem was first published in *Sehnsucht*.

"Nocturne with Monkey"—begins with a Lewis quote from "Dogma and the Universe" which appears in *God in the Dock* (p. 41). Both Pascal's *Pensées* and monkeys are spoken of in the essay. This poem was first published in *Anglican Theological Review*, and has subsequently also appeared in *Ancient Paths*.

"Thirst"—is my interaction in support of an argument from chapter five of *The Great Divorce* (p. 44 of my Macmillian paperback). The italicized words appear in Lewis's book.

"On a Summer's Day"—reflects on a concept from the essay "Democratic Education", in the Harcourt collection *Present Concerns* (p. 34). The italicized words in my poem are Lewis's.

"About the Feeder"—is inspired by the Lewis poem "Eden's Courtesy" from *Poems*.

"The Abolition of Man"—is drawn from the book of the same name (p. 48). This poem was first published in *Convivium*.

"Moon Landing"—comes from a point made in "On Stories" in *Of This & Other Worlds* (p. 36). The short story "Forms of Things Unknown" from *The Dark Tower* (Fount, p. 132) is an illustration of the same idea.

"Life on Other Planets"—is inspired by a line from "Religion & Rocketry" in *Fern-seeds and Elephants* (p. 93). Lewis also explores this idea in the first two novels in his space trilogy.

"Flamboyance"—comes out of a line Lewis wrote in the preface to the third edition of *The Pilgrim's Regress* (Eerdmans, p.10). The line is italicized in the poem. This poem was first published in *The Christian Century*.

"In the Shelterless Street"—is about a feeling Lewis describes (on page 106) of "The Weight of Glory" from *Screwtape Proposes a Toast: and other pieces*.

"To Know"—begins with a quote from "Man or Rabbit?" in *God in the Dock* (p.108)." By page 111 he speaks of honest and dishonest error; the poem springboards from that point.

"Passage"—features a Lewis quote—interrupted and resumed—from an illustration in *Mere Christianity* (p. 143). There's also an allusion to T.S. Eliot's *Four Quartets*, despite Lewis's early dislike of Eliot's poetry. This poem was first published in *Relief*.

"Piano Lesson"—comes from an illustration Lewis uses in *Mere Christianity* (page 22 in my Fount paperback) in the chapter "Some Objections." This poem was first published in *Windhover*.

"Democracy"—grew from the Lewis idea at the end of the poem. It comes from "Equality" in the Harcourt collection *Present Concerns*.

"After Evensong"—relates to the Lewis poem "Evensong" in *Poems*. The italicized words are from his poem.

"Waiting"—is based on "a faint analogy" in the paper "On Obstinacy in Belief" from *Screwtape Proposes a Toast* (p. 71). This poem was first published in *Convivium*.

"Truth in Myth"—is inspired by one of Lewis's letters to Arthur Greeves, which I found quoted in *The Narnian* (p. 148ff). These ideas are expressed elsewhere as well, such as in *Surprised by Joy* (p. 55, and 188–89). This poem was first published in *Dappled Things*.

"On the Latest Impending Doom"—relates to the Lewis poem "On the Atomic Bomb" in *Poems*. The italicized words are from his poem.

"The Great Divorce"—is my creative summarizing of the book *The Great Divorce*. This poem was first published in *Sehnsucht*.

"Wisdom from Malcandra"—is, as the subtitle states, "a glimpse into the space trilogy of C.S. Lewis"; in this case it is from the first novel, *Out of the Silent Planet* (Scribner Classics). This poem, and the two which follow, were displayed as part of a gallery exhibition in conjunction with the Colloquium—in Oxford, England—for the presentation of *Perelandra—The Opera*, in June 2009.

"Innocence of Perelandra"—is a glimpse into the novel, *Perelandra* (Scribner Classics)—a.k.a. *Voyage to Venus*. For poem publication history see the above note for "Wisdom from Malcandra."

"The Somnambulist"—is about the character, the Deputy Director, in *That Hideous Strength* (Scribner Classics) which is the final novel in Lewis's space trilogy. For poem publication history see the above note for "Wisdom from Malcandra."

"What Lucy Saw"—is inspired by the novel *Prince Caspian* (HarperCollins), particularly chapter nine. This poem was first published in *Mythic Circle*.

"A Parliament of Owls"—relates to the fourth chapter of Lewis's fourth Narnia book—*The Silver Chair* (HarperCollins). Incidentally some publishers number the books according to chronology in the story, however it makes more sense to read them in the order in which they were first published. This poem was first published in *The Lamp-Post*.

"Contemplation"—comes from the chapter "Across the Canyon by Moonlight" in The Pilgrim's Regress (Eerdmans, p. 121).

"The Shove & Tumble"—is written from the perspective of the demon Screwtape as seen in letter XIV of *The Screwtape Letters* (Fontanta, p.71ff).

"Among the Tombs"—is based on a scene in chapter six of the Narnia book—*The Horse and His Boy* (HarperCollins).

"Aping Presence"—is a reflection on the final Narnia book—*The Last Battle* (HarperCollins).

"Psalm of Incarnation"—is inspired by a quote in the introductory section of *Reflections on the Psalms* (p. 12) where Lewis says, "It seems to me appropriate, almost inevitable, that when the great Imagination . . . submitted to express Itself in human speech, that speech should sometimes be poetry. For poetry too is a little incarnation, giving body to what had been before invisible and inaudible."

"The Death of Words"—comes from the C.S. Lewis essay "The Death of Words" from the book *Of This & Other Worlds* (p. 138ff). The opening line comes from the Lewis poem "Re-Adjustment" from *Poems*.

"Winterlake"—is projected, as I've said, from a line in the C.S. Lewis poem "Pattern" from *Poems*.

"The Silence of One Voice" — is drawn from "Five Sonnets" in *Poems*. This poem was first published in *Relief*.

"Undergrowth"—concludes with the same final line as Lewis's poem "Footnote To All Prayers" from *Poems*.

"The Atlantic"—is introduced with the beginning of a quote from *Mere Christianity* (p.131–32). "In the same way, if a man has once looked at the Atlantic from the beach, and then goes and looks at a map of the Atlantic, he also will be turning from something real to something less real . . ." Lewis then goes on to compare theology to a map. This poem was first published in *Relief*.

"Tumbled By the Surf"—relates to a comment by Lewis in *The Four Loves* (p. 120). This poem was first published in *Sehnsucht*.

"Apologetics"—refers to Lewis's famous "proof" for Christ's deity in *Mere Christianity* (p. 52), which is also turned into an analogy in *The Lion, The Witch and the Wardrobe* (HarperCollins, p. 48). The introductory quote is from "God Believes in You" from the album *Everything Matters* by the songwriter Pierce Pettis (1998 Compass Records).

"Lion"—is from a scene in *The Voyage of The Dawn Treader.* (HarperCollins).

"Ghost Ship"—comes out of my imagining of a scene leaping from a passing comment in the chapter, "Scripture," from *Reflections on the Psalms* (p. 94).

"Wick"—is drawn from the sermon "The Weight of Glory" as found in *Screwtape Proposes a Toast: and other pieces* (p. 102).

"The Vocation of Maples"—grew out of the following quote: "To follow the vocation does not mean happiness: but once it has been heard, there is no happiness for those who do not follow." It is taken from the chapter "Virgil and the Subject of Secondary Epic" in the book *A Preface To Paradise Lost* (p. 38–39).

"Plastic Flute"—is my expansion from a Lewis analogy in the sermon "Transposition" as published in *Screwtape Propose a Toast: and other pieces* (p. 92). This poem was first published in *Sehnsucht*.

"Signature"—is inspired by the chapter "Heaven" in *The Problem of Pain* (p. 134ff). This poem was first published in *Penwood Review*.

"Destination"—leaps out of an illustration in *Mere Christianity* (p. 144).